Let us begin by declaring that Peggy Robles-Alvarado is a magic maker. Her poetry plows under your skin until you feel your soul brimming with epiphanies. In *Burn Me Back*, Robles-Alvarado invites us to party with the machinations of truth-telling, and no matter how much you try to avert its gaze, there is enough lyric, enough innovative turn of phrase, enough history, enough fire, enough celestial invocation, enough family lore to make you a believer in rebirth, in salvaging what is left in the aftermath of a lineage fractured by secrets. If you ever doubted poetry's ability to make you whole, welcome to this sublime reckoning.
—Willie Perdomo, *The Crazy Bunch*

Peggy Robles-Alvarado's *Burn Me Back* sings with the gale force of Oyá and Guabancex, its verbivocovisual spell encompassing fractured lyric narrative, performance score, experimental process writing, concrete poetry, and Afro-Latina testimonio. Come for the rhythmic dazzle, fierce wit, Spanglish glyphs, and mujerista erotics, and stay for the diasporic world-building, rooted in working class New York Puerto Rican and Dominican histories and all their hard-earned wisdom. This book is unflinching in its reckoning with cross-generational violence and trauma as they connect to patriarchy, colonialism, and displacement, yet it also claims the performalist power (translingual acrostics, yo!) to forge a somatic language as untranslatable and expansive as our bodyminds ("reteach my bones to speak survival"). Robles-Alvarado is an essential figure in Nueva York poetry and performance and *Burn Me Back* is her best work yet, a virtuosic primer on survival as a shared creative practice of "liberación and pleasure" that demands new ways of reading and meaning.
—Urayoán Noel, Writer, Translator, and Performer.

We want. And that want blisters within us. Peggy Robles-Alvarado's profoundly hopeful book, *Burn Me Back*, finds a steady beat (el son, la clave) of the fires within us: what we light to dispose of, what lights within us. She teaches me to discern, to write beyond my own limits and the limits of a poem, where the world scorches in its memory. These exceptional poems of life, for life, are a dress of fire and ashes for all of us who want to learn our own geography, who want to keep us safe and save ourselves, who feed each other that tenderness among our own fires.
—Ricardo Maldonado, *The Life Assignment*

Peggy Robles-Alvarado's new collection, *Burn Me Back*, is a testament to the epidemic of American colonial sicknesses enacted over generations in the Caribbean and its diasporas and the strength it takes to heal. Though she begins the collection with her father's alcoholism, she does not end there, taking us on a familial and personal journey of migration, economic exploitation, anti-blackness, misogyny, xenophobia, (mis)education, pressures of assimilation, sexual assault, loss, and restoration. Perhaps Robles-Alvarado's most personal collection yet for a poet who is no stranger to vulnerability, each poem in the collection pulls you forward with her unique mix of narrative, intoxicating imagery, and metaphor. In poems that also show mastery of various poetic forms, you are in the delivery room, the living room, the schoolyard, and the sweatshop. You will both want to rush forward to the next poem and linger indefinitely, in order to fully savor and grasp lines about home, language, gender, grief, and more. The most stunning poetry collection I have read in many years, this will immediately be a centerpiece of my teaching.
—Dr. Melissa Castillo-Garsow, Associate Professor of English, Lehman College & Graduate Center, CUNY, and author of the award-winning collection, *Chingona Rules*.

Burn Me Back is a poetry collection that I've been eagerly waiting for. These poems are petroglyphs etched by a poet who knows something about brown girls made from fire. From Santiago, DR to Puerto Rico to the Bronx, Robles-Alvarado's searing verses unearth matrilineal lineages across borders, gendered bodies, and bloodlines. What we hear is the weight of it all through the tender eyes of a daughter making sense of the world around her. In one poem she writes, "My tongue: / always the unsteady bridge / for an immigrant mother who waits / for me to explain / if my country will allow her / to call it home too." Using repetition as a spell to undo and reclaim, I felt myself pulled into the mouth of inherited stories as Robles-Alvarado explores which ones to keep and which ones to let burn. Simply put, this is a collection I'll be living alongside for a long time.
—Denice Frohman, Poet and Performer

Burn Me Back

Burn Me Back

Peggy Robles-Alvarado

Four Way Books
Tribeca

Dedicated to every kid
who survived
family parties
where the grown-ups drank too much,

and to all the kids
who didn't

This book is manufactured in the United States of America and printed on acid-free paper.

Library of Congress Cataloging-in-Publication Data

Names: Robles-Alvarado, Peggy, author.
Title: Burn me back / Peggy Robles-Alvarado.
Other titles: Burn me back (Compilation)
Description: Tribeca : Four Way Books, 2025.
Identifiers: LCCN 2025003843 (print) | LCCN 2025003844 (ebook) | ISBN 9781961897663 (trade paperback) | ISBN 9781961897670 (ebook)
Subjects: LCGFT: Poetry.
Classification: LCC PS3618.O3364 B87 2025 (print) | LCC PS3618.O3364 (ebook) | DDC 811/.6--dc23/eng/20250210
LC record available at https://lccn.loc.gov/2025003843
LC ebook record available at https://lccn.loc.gov/2025003844

Four Way Books is a not-for-profit literary press. We are grateful for the assistance we receive from individual donors, public arts agencies, and private foundations including the New York State Council on the Arts, a state agency.

We are a proud member of the Community of Literary Magazines and Presses.

Contents

I Light

II Slow Burn

III Glow

I
Light

Coke No Rum

—After Warsan Shire

This is where I want to start
him: limber
picking himself up off the bedroom floor
His heartbeat: steady
The sensation of nerves in his left arm: a lullaby
The shot glass presses away from his lips
The last of a half-empty bottle of Bacardi 151
sitting by the kitchen table
for the rest of his life—
                                        that's how we bring Papi back.
I can make his skin supple again,
drain the bilirubin from his eyes,
color his liver a healthy slick of brown,
make his stool bloodless
Pull the spiked Coke from the drain, serve it to guests
No vomit speckling the floor like hell's night sky
Papi will sing décimas on key with Tío Enrique
strumming a sober guitar and maybe I joy-cry
out of love this time, so much love
I can write this, make his whole life reappear.

I can write this, make his whole life reappear.
out of love this time, so much love
strumming a sober guitar and maybe I joy-cry
Papi will sing décimas on key with Tío Enrique
no vomit speckling the floor like hell's night sky
Pull the spiked Coke from the drain, serve it to guests
make his stool bloodless
color his liver a healthy slick of brown,
drain the bilirubin from his eyes,
I can make his skin supple again,
                    that's how we bring Papi back.
for the rest of his life—
sitting by the kitchen table
The last of a half-empty bottle of Bacardi 151
The shot glass presses away from his lips
The sensation of nerves in his left arm: a lullaby
His heartbeat: steady
picking himself up off the bedroom floor
him: limber
This is where I want to start

Dandelions

After spring rainstorms
dandelions bloomed in every sidewalk,
all disrespectful—unwanted—never seeking acceptance.
True of any invasive species, just wanting to lay roots
in the patchy grass of busy roadsides, on the banks
of polluted city rivers, pushing up haphazard yellow
in the most expensively dull green lawns where the rich
admonish them intrusive weeds. Banish them to mulch,
drowned in pesticide, choking the stem—
attempting to collapse the life cycle.

Mami picked dandelions from High Bridge Park.
Plucked them perky and persistent
growing between a rainbow of empty crack vials.
Like any good immigrant wife,
she looked for streets paved with gold
and for now, this herb would do.
Made Papi tea to clear his liver, mixed it with olive oil
to soothe hives, placed bundles on the windowsill
facing the nosey neighbor to quiet gossip.

Taught me:
Even the most undesirable things can be celestial.

The flower: a sun.
The seeds so easily dispersed: stars.
The puff sphere: a full moon.

She tells me:
When they say you don't belong
persist,
take a deep breath,
and make a wish.

What They Mean By Papers

Papeles:
Not the *Daily News* or *El Diario La Prensa*,
or the kind my mother read to me on Sunday
mornings. Her voice, raspy, a throat full of
pelitos de mango making sure to read each article
twice so that maybe I wouldn't reject Spanish
as fiercely as she had rejected English.
Our tongues disloyal to new soil. Patriots only
to the papers and sounds we were familiar with,
the paper that could feed us: money and the prayers
written on them tucked under the mattress.
Cause who trusted banks anyway?

Papeles:
Not the kind Tía Weltina used to roll her tobacco with.
The smell of her neatly constructed cigars conjuring
Taíno spirits she exhaled out the fire escape window
as she tried to memorize the national anthem. Studying
for her citizenship exam in a language that didn't sound
as soothing as the rain hitting her zinc rooftop back
in Santiago. The smoke twirling around vowels
and consonants. Her mouth struggling to articulate
the heaviness of a language too comfortable with conquest.
Wasn't it enough that her grandmother's tongue

was believed extinct and there were only two ways
of saying *I love you* in Spanish?

Papeles:
The kind that convinced four of my aunts to marry older
naturalized men in exchange for an acre of my grandfather's
campo. The barter of one fertile untouched land for another
promised to be paved in gold. The payment: their bodies,
all their milk and honey, all their amber and caña dulce
sacrificed to the lust of viejos verdes, old bastards
who soured early on too much tabaco y ron and wanted to plant
their moldy seeds in supple girls who had never seen snow.
How important was consent when there were
so many mouths to feed?

Papeles:
The kind my Uncle Rito forged. Placed his dead brother's name
on every dotted line. Learned to curl the R in his name
as if writing sacred geometry. Always that ghost perched
on his back. The weight hunching his shoulders,
hardening his eyes. His real name Julio, reduced
to an unfamiliar nickname he only responded to on Saturdays
during domino games and shots of Mamajuana with other men
whose wives were still stretched across the ocean awaiting a visa.

The illusion of living his best life written in the few letters
he sent back home with seventy-five dollars to help feed his two kids.
Even if he had to share a room with four other men, he was still
the only one in his family to own more than one pair of shoes.

When Mami Talks About Going Sober For The First Time

I could have poured myself
into shots of anisette-again.
Until the whites of my eyes
were set to sunshine-again.

Until bittersweet bile made my knees
seesaw through town
looking for someone to gather
all this piecework made skin
and flesh-again.

To pull shatter from me
until I got back to myself-again.
But rum and I had swaggered and sashayed
into suffering too many times. I swore it off
at least until I met your father.

Pressed my lips to his blaze
found a familiar warmth.
A fire we both set on simmer

just to get through the day but
he burned enough for the both of us.

Your father feared my lust.
A want that stemmed
from fermented fruit
turned chaotic brew.

No man can really handle
all that ripe, all that *dame*
tied to a corkscrew
and bitter aftertaste.

So, I prayed through the night sweats
and seizures until the throb in my veins
stopped calling on the raspy lover
at the bottom of that bottle.

I whispered myself full until-alone
I became enough to pretend

I could stir all this ache
into pots of asopao
and call it-ternura.

I made room for a child,
thinking a baby could suckle
a mother out of all this imperfect,
bless this body as a first home
and pull at the Gods to teach me
how to become refuge
for the both of us.

Swelter

—After Eduardo C. Corral

Six months pregnant,
my mother, right leg
an engorged eggplant
pressing the foot pedal,
withering under pounds
of lace piece work, beaded
appliqué, plastic rose buttons,
threading needles, MADE IN
THE USA tags, 13 hour shift,
doors chained shut to ensure
productivity, her tongue
a cracked road in Santiago
during a drought, yellowing
paper towels balled between
breasts and underarms,
her cheeks red like the apples
in her purse, a ten minute lunch
marked by a defunct clock, air
thicker than the accents begging
for clean water, her throat
full of want.

The summer my tongue traced
his belt buckle, I finally understood
that kind of heat.

What I Hear When Papi Tells My Birth Story

The soul doesn't fully enter a newborn body
until it's ushered into the lungs by a first breath—
twenty one grams settle into ripe bronchi.

The flames of burning stardust steady a heartbeat
and the uprooting of past lives begins with
a blunt chant sung to the rise and fall of the chest.

But you were still
unfinished
and tempting return.

The souls of severed kin fought displacement by carving throb
and ache into your drying palms.
Slyly, they cooed emancipation,
demanded you reach for them, before the umbilical cord was cut.

Gasping between white light and midnight,
your mother's body became unsteady weather
of howling wind and bursting periphery.

Her hiccupped heartbeat quickly fading as she fought
the colors back into their lines. Her own twenty-one grams
razored, tangled in war cry.

It was the fading heart monitor that rocked me explosive.

Fist pounding drywall was the sound that pulled your mother back into her body as she stretched for all the God in you.

Dolores, Altagracia, Carmen, María

All of my Tías inherited the same four names arranged differently
on birth certificates filed months after their actual births.
No attention paid to zodiac signs or temperaments.
No tenderness considered when the first girl
was born with high cheekbones

that could scorch the earth like a Rita and not a Carmen, ready to plant
a quiet garden of wall flowers. No coddling for the fourth girl,
whose wails announced threatening storms with the whirlwind
of a Sophia and not the church hymns whispered
during the passionless, muted births of every María.

No nine-day respite or eulogies to retire the sorrow of the name given
to the seventh girl who failed to take her first breath. Her body—
the same hue of violet as the dress she was buried in. Like her bassinet,
her name—still warm, offered to the lips of the next girl
Abuela unwillingly freed from her womb.

Abuelo's lust detached from the consequences of too many mouths
to feed, too many names to remember, too many vowels to perch
on a tongue made jagged by sharp consonants. The same four names,
revolving biblical placeholders, awaiting the opulent surnames
that would make

having all these girls
worth it.

Naming (or Why I Don't Sound Like A Peggy)

Anamaría Lucía

María Dolores Ana Dolores

María Carmen Ana Carmen

Peggy

María Altagracia Altagracia Carmen

María Mercedes Lucía Mercedes

Lucía María

"You sound like ______"

you should go back where you came from una presentá YOU DON'T KNOW WHERE HOME IS SPANGLISH

no sabes tu propio nombre

you don't belong una estupida you are not from

una mal educada NON-ENGLISH Dolores una presentá

una tíguera NON-SPANISH Altagracia Nuyorican

una freca María IMMIGRANT Carmen

una Bori dolor español de la calle

María Lucía STREET-SPANISH Mercedes Altagracia María

Anamaría Dolores Ana María Lucía una hija de tu madre

María NON-ENGLISH

you don't belong here una estupida

una mal educada Ana una freca Dolores una sucia

una Dominican York

María Dolores an immigrant You have an accent una mal paría

go home gringa a mutt NON-SPANISH

a mutt una chamaquita MIGRANT

María Ana una mal paría una mal paría

NON-ENGLISH Ana

Carmen Dolores dolor es IMMIGRANT dolor

go home gringa MIGRANT María

dolor una Bori Mercedes María

español de la calle Ana Dolores You have an accent

a mutt SPANGLISH

una Dominican York

By The Time We Are Seven

Our Tías teach us to clip our noses
with a clothespin. We become
mouth breathers as they pray
our faces don't grow to be
like our grandmother's—
wide and welcoming, brown
and full-bodied. Our broad nasal bone
and cartilage: a pyramid.

In social studies, I read ancient Egyptians
thought the pyramids to be a way
for the physical body to ascend
towards the sun. That is to say,
this mound of flesh at the center of my face
be a compass to the heavens. And I always knew
my grandmother, and her coffee-kissed skin,
was closer to God than any of her daughters.

My Tías, who rubbed lemon wedges
on our dark spots and kept us from tanning.
Who bought magazines with pale models
pointing their perky little noses at the camera
making the mirror our enemy.

In science, I read the nose is responsible
for the sound of your voice. The richness
of its tone determined by vibrations
in the larynx and gusts of air rushed
from the lungs. The same principle
that divides a clarinet from a kazoo.

When you pinch your nose in the name of beauty,
you surrender your voice for the sake
of your Tia's approval. You grow to learn
that a quiet mouth with a kazoo
caught in its teeth
can make that unruly nose of yours
just a little prettier.

When You're The One In The House That Speaks English

¿Qué dice? Mami demanded,
pulling at the coloring book
and scented markers pressed to my chest
replacing them with today's mail.
My third-grade English trembling
at the sight of legal paper and torn
envelope, eyes watering, our reflections
caught in the silver seal pressed
into the paper, the branding of an official
document, a new border, Mami's tongue:
an unclassified animal caught in this
barbed wire of menacing font and formality,
mocking the block letters and static penmanship
of her copied signature at the bottom of the page.

Twirling the crucifix dangling from her neck
between index and thumb, she tries to summon
a God of letters to calm the slow rise
of a rage fueled by uncertainty, as I stumble
line by line, heaving, trying to craft my own spell,
to mend sounds to symbols.

English, then Spanish, then Mami.
English, then Spanish, then

the Spanish Mami and I speak at home.
English then Spanish, then heart, then Mami.
English, then Spanish, then heart, then
blank, a void, a gap in understanding.
I decode, decode, squint, decode,
repeat the sounds to fill spaces
with what I hope Mami wants me to say.

This is more than a school memo,
a notice from the power company,
another denial for public assistance
on a technicality. My tongue:
always the unsteady bridge
for an immigrant mother who waits
for me to explain
if my country will allow her
to call it home too.

Dique A Glosa En Merengue For Mami

Qué pena y qué dolor, qué manera de sufrir
Es la primera vez que te vas de mi
Madre mia, deja de llorar, que muy pronto quiero regresar
Voy en busca de mi porvenir, y una vida digna; digna para ti
—“Madre Mia” por Sergio Vargas

Sergio Vargas’s voice echoed from the kitchen/Mami rewound
the cassette/delicately untangling it with a pencil’s eraser/
the radio threatening to swallow the song on replay/pulling at
the rollers/turning the cassette reel/the brown ribbon recoiled/
anxiously reinserting the tape into the player/Sergio sang
the soundtrack to an intimate sorrow/only pots and pans witnessed/
Qué pena y qué dolor, qué manera de sufrir

Between swigs of Löwenbräu beer/singing along to each verse/secretly
I watched from the doorway/tears soaking her blouse/an immigrant
story emerging between chorus and bridge/the day she left Santiago/
stopping Abuelo from beating Abuela bloody for not serving breakfast/
after pulling the gun from his holster/after the threat at his chest/
Abuela’s plea soft as a cigua palmera/a trembling farewell/
Es la primera vez que te vas de mi

Fingers tapping on the table/Sergio's voice same as the day she arrived/
rewinding the tape/rewinding the day/drinking another beer/cold
New York City winter/dress shoes sinking in snow/her sister's
overcrowded apartment/her sister's frowning husband/no heat/no
hot water/no English/no dirt roads/no dulce de leche/one telephone/
one call/one-word answers to Abuela's questions/
the pulling back of tears/
Madre mia deja de llorar, que muy pronto quiero regresar

Again the radio stops/the tape stuck/Mami's fingers made more clumsy
after a third bottle/rewind/fast forward/tape taut again/the song playing
again/snowfall again/a job/a sweatshop/a sewing machine/
a pedal/an engorged leg/cash in hand/cash wired to Santiago/pesos
in Abuela's hands/dólares under Mami's mattress/days repeat/
days rewind but don't fast forward/the telephone rings/
Abuela's voice/a bird searching for its wings/Mami answers
Voy en busca de mi porvenir, y una vida digna; digna para ti

(As)s(i)mil(ate)

The kids bring:
superhero lunch bags bulging
with Doritos/25¢ juices/Fun Dip/
one slice of cheese smothered
between two pieces of soft
Wonder Bread/Oreos crumbling
in Ziplocs

I bring:
A plastic bag smelling of mangú
con salami sweating in a Parkay
container turned Tupperware/a fork
Mami tells me I better not
lose/morir soñando curdling
in Papi's red thermos

The kids:
trade blue and red sugar water/cool ranch
for spicy nacho/cringe at the oil and onions
sliding down my mound of plantain mash

I:

eat/alone.

leave

the bag.

learn to

lose.

How We Learned Geography

Came to believe my mother's geography was a
fantasy or crazy or at least too old-fashioned
—Audre Lorde

The girls slow ride
pink bikes with fringed
handlebars, zigzag
on glittering roller skates
trying to avoid cracks
in weathered hallway tiles
and find places to hide
and seek within long
narrow corridors of our
apartment building.
                    They learn to play inside.
                                        Use their imaginations
                                        to freeze frame into doorways.
                                        Ball their bodies under stairwells,
                                        emergency-stop elevators,
                                        learn to jump three times
                                        when it slows between
                                        the fourth and fifth floor.
                                        The only windows that open

face other buildings, watching
other girls, reach and stretch,
poking limbs through metal bars
in fire escape staircases
to share Bubble Yum and toss
jump rope handles, making them
circle and clip the wind in swirls.
Between alleyways, girls
tether themselves to each other
for a moment until the rope falls
and they watch it take temporary
flight in a show of freedom,
then drop on wide mouthed
garbage cans that swallow toys,
dirty diapers and used condoms.
They learn to play inside
until Mami's nod waves them
safely home long before sunset.

How They Learned Geography

The boys
freestyle on BMX bikes
fast pedal through foot
traffic on Amsterdam
scaring Abuelitas who drop handbags
and yell
¡Hijos de su madre!
laugh loud and shoot
phlegm onto Audubon sidewalks
j-hop for the girls who start
wearing lipstick this year
wipe sweat from their foreheads
on the sleeves of their graphic T-shirts
ride from High Bridge to
Dyckman stopping only to gulp
water from open fire hydrants or rub dirt on knees
scraped by sidewalks after failing
a 180 off the curb or
to buy tamarindo
flavored piraguas whose empty plastic cups
they toss at each other before
popping
wheelies down St. Nicholas
until the sun

sets and
signals the
way
home

Ode To The Plastic Cover On The Sofa

Oh you thick coat of sweat-inducing armor
for Victorian-styled seating purchased
after months of saving money under the
mattress and in empty cans of Bustelo.

Casing for curved wooden accents and
gold laurel wreaths delicately sewn into
each cushion and armrest that could be
seen but never touched.

Sheath wiped clean with Windex after
slippery beer cans and evidence of
spontaneous sex rained on back pillows
that never lost their shape.

Best friend of the rocking chair imported
from Santiago that once sat in a marquesina
now facing the television and radiola paid
for by Papi's side hustle of la bolita.

Sworn enemy of the impractical slipcover
that couldn't take a hit of a lit cigarette,
Mami's ruby red Covergirl lipstick
or a spill of Country Club Soda.

Oh glorious, transparent protector that
yellowed and crinkled over time.
Oh rigid, synthetic luxury, that taught
our bodies to adjust to your heat,

praise be your lessons in learning to
sit still, sweat, peel off, and repeat.

At Every Family Party Where The Grown-ups Drank Too Much

We knew we inherited these mouths.
Forced openings of treacherous scowls,
all crooked-toothed and salivating,
descendants of Caribs, dressed in pink tulle and lace.
Too much lip, too much tongue to keep quiet.
Too much bite to let them run their dirty fingers over our
half-smiles, knowing drunk uncles weren't just wiping off
our little girl grins, they wanted us dirty.
Wanted to choke out the pulsing of war cry pressing
at our underdeveloped chests. Wanted to reteach our jaws
to open wide in surrender. But we: daughters of savages,
surnamed chaos, learned to dance for Guabancex before
they baptized her María. We: spit rituals of rupture
into their half-finished Solo cups, trying to reverse the root,
unwilling to justify the ache.
We: the niñas bonitas pero malcriadas, renamed
what they wanted to call silence—explosive.

Sábados De Gloria In Haiku

Awake before nine,
speakers singing merengue—
weekly ritual.

Prayers for our home
Mistolín, holy water
and Fabuloso.

Gloria mops the floor.
Her hips sway to el coro
de Fernandito.

Moving furniture
to get to all the corners,
she lights a cigar.

Clouds each room with smoke,
says Lord's prayer between tracks.
Here, God dances too.

Washing away sin
by day, and drinking all night—
a game of seesaw.

Our home: a temple
for both heathen and holy
with beer on their breath.

How I Learned Not To Fear The Dark

After we posed behind the family dinner table
adorned with plastic candy bags
wearing cone-shaped hats,
after the heavily frosted cake was cut
and served on paper plates,
after the long party balloons taped to the wall
were popped in a battle between
girls in ruffle dresses and boys in polyester pants,
the adults declared the party theirs.
My cousins and I,
riding the last few minutes of a day's long sugar high,
settled into Tía's bed where layers of leather
and faux fur coats served as comforters,
Duérmete, que a esta hora sale El Cuco.

El Cuco*:* a shapeless male figure
that roamed the night looking to kidnap children
who interrupted their parents
as they danced merengue in cramped living rooms,
who knew when we said *coño* under our breath,
and when we sneaked long drags of Mami's cigarette
causing our chests to hollow for days.
Maybe he roamed at night because he was a Sagittarius

like me, the feral child of the zodiac
who sat on the fire escape watching the heat rise
from the asphalt and the older boys gather
in the corner after sunset.

Maybe like me, El Cuco can't sleep.
Knows Tío always checks to see if our eyes are closed,
glides his thick fingers over my lips
until I show him my teeth and
pierce the drunken laughter in the next room
with a scream that says I too am part shadow.
Tío renames me—*¡Muchacha 'el diablo!* stumbling backwards
into the pulsing of strobe lights Tía turned on after midnight.

Maybe El Cuco took sips of Papi's Heineken
when he wasn't looking,
or put gum in Coochi's hair
when she didn't share the Skittles in her goodie bag.
I bet El Cuco laughed
when I made Lila drink toilet water in Truth or Dare.
Maybe El Cuco is lonely.
Maybe he just wants to dance bachata with La Llorona

when no one sees him
after too many shots of Brugal.

Maybe El Cuco is impatient like me.
Knows these parties always end too late
to pour out the last beer
that will pull the rising hurt from Papi's chest
into an explosion that will flip tables,
draw daggers from Mami's eyes,
pool saliva in the corners of slurred mouths
ready to snap.

El Cuco knows the sunrise fades
the memory of adults who ruin children's birthday parties.
He laughs as the grown-ups stumble over thick tongues
and swallow apologies like cold beer to kill a hangover.

Maybe I am El Cuco, learning never to fear the dark.
Learning to dig graves in these wrists—
my collection of party favors.

Sonnet In Case Tío Chucho Brings Brugal To The Party

—After Ariel Dorfman

Start praying/Remember not to fall asleep even if all your cousins cradle into piles of coats/Make sure to keep an eye on his cup/Pour it out the window or lean it into the closest potted plant when he steady grinds into a second merengue with Tía Lila/Avoid group photos if it means you must sit on his lap/Pray/Remember you have always been his favorite/ Now you see how shouting will not help in a living room where everyone slurs too loud/Stay low/Keep praying as his face loosens puddles of drool into the crescents of his mouth/Keep an eye on the door or the fire escape/Watch his eyes shadow/Since the age of five you have always been his favorite/I told you

start praying

Domingos De Recuperación In Haiku

Stale beer, dry vomit
staining the linoleum,
waking half past noon.

To recuperate,
Mami starts the sancocho,
Tía makes café.

The men: still sleeping
on the loveseat or the floor.
Kids: up since seven

want pancakes, not soup.
Regret settles in the broth.
Sober with sadness,

the women break day,
hum to last night's boleros,
chain-smoke Marlboros.

No one goes to church.
Sundays are for hangovers
chased by ginger ale.

Here, God is summoned
in bowls of soft viandas.
¡Dios, qué sabroso!

How I Learned Not To Smile

The women in my family never smiled in pictures.

Stoic faces framed by bouffant or pompadour hair stiffened by Aqua Net and years of learning to tolerate the dry heat of salon hair dryers and marriages that lasted too long. Saving face required red or pink lips. Soft parallel lines turned beautiful barbed wire trained to hold tongues, clenched teeth and swallow the suffering that came with the gossip of children that lived on the other side of the city but looked just like their husbands. Boleros hummed from a heart that drowned in whiskey all that was sour and renamed it satisfaction. Manicured hands gently perched under a powdered chin, neatly folded on a skirted lap or restless on the hips of high waisted jeans.

¡Cuidado, que los perros andan sueltos!

they warned,

posing for photos only the men wanted to take.

The men in my family always smiled in pictures.

Toothy grins, exposing poor dental work, done too late to
save incisors or premolars from porcelain caps or gold crowns.
Their cheeks flushed by the kind of laughter that comes from
Budweisers chilled in bathtubs filled with ice or the high-
pitched whine of a guitar in old school bachata they sang
along to, or the children they hid from this family gathering.
A chorus of sweat dripping from pomade and polyester. Arms
entangled in necks, leaning on shoulders, fists up in fighting
stance, lit cigarettes perched on purpled lips.
¡Parecemos perros!
they chuckled after rolls of film and
polaroids were developed and protected behind plastic sleeves
in photo albums only the women collected.

Learning To Cook

Tía Leticia, Tía Luz, Tía Altagracia, and Tía Dolores
all came to New York by marrying viejos verdes.
Their late teens and early twenties spent learning
to fake orgasms at night and smiles during the day.

Gathered in the kitchen, smoking Newport Lights,
drinking Löwenbräus straight from the bottle,
like the men did, they mocked each other's husbands.
The way their tightened belts struggled to keep their pants up
underneath round hardened beer bellies.
Men who thought themselves roosters strutting
around the block on weekends, flaunting factory jobs
they cursed each night for back pain and arthritic hands.

Lip syncing to *Las Chicas del Can,* dreaming of owning
manicured hands and lawns, desperate for the love affairs
of telenovelas watched every evening, they framed American
dreams with alcohol and picturesque snowfalls that mercilessly
soaked their second-hand spring jackets and ruined shoes
that stumbled into brown puddles of ice water.

The kitchen: their safe house, keeper of secrets, a respite
for lives in waiting, where my Tías fed their men

and learned to starve themselves, drinking just enough
to remind their hearts that hunger can make the most bitter,
sweet.

When I Became La Promesa

For every unexpected illness that required medical insurance, every second-trimester miscarriage, every chaos unemployment caused, every looming eviction, every arrest warrant gone unanswered, the women in my family made promesas to plaster cast statues worshipped in overcrowded apartments with rum poured over linoleum, nine-day candles coughing black soot until the wick surrendered, Florida water perfuming doorways and the backs of necks.

Promesas: barters, contracts with a God they didn't vow to change for but always appeased. Bowls of fruit, paper bags filled with coconut candy and cacerolas de ajiaco left at busy intersections, an oak tree in High Bridge Park, the doorway of the 34th precinct, and, when mar pacífico and rompe saragüey refused to grow on Washington Heights windowsills, the youngest became part of the trade.

Unsullied and unaware, cousin Mari pissed about having to dress in green and red for twenty-one days to keep Tío Pablo out of jail. Luisito scratching at an anklet made of braided corn silk to help Tía Lorna find a new job, and my hair not to be cut until Papi's tumor was removed. Gathered in tight buns or sectioned pigtails, falling long past my waist when asymmetrical bobs were in fashion. Not knowing my crown had the necessary coercion to dislodge a mass from a colon, I grabbed my older brother's clippers, ran thirsty blades across my right temple to the back of my ear, massaged the softness that emerged as strands were abandoned on bathroom tiles. My desire to mimic freestyle icons, whose albums my cousins and I scratched on old record players, wagered against Papi's large intestine.

My unsteady hand: a fist in the face of God.

Bachata Para El Atardecer

—Remezcla from Washington Heights of "A Hymn to the Evening" by Phillis Wheatley Peters

Coochi and I dangled our legs over the fire escape
watching the orange sherbet sky slump to a drunken violet
as the pigeons and house sparrows disappeared
into tight spaces of surrounding rooftops.
Their mingled music floating alongside the smoke
of Coochi's cigarette stolen from Tía's purse.
The incense of blooming spring, a last puff
of a Newport, wet concrete signaling the lack
of trees on our street, the thunder announcing rain
like the high-pitched guitar in the bachata songs on replay.

one two three pa' rriba
one two three pa' rriba
Que vuelva, que vuelva

Untuned voices breaking night,
celebrating everything that made us
less heav'nly, less refin'd.

Stumbling between stairs and an open window,
right hand on our hearts, left hand thirsting

for el tíguere in apartment 3C.
Our breasts hunched and howling the lyrics
of a heart bleeding the deepest red
into Solo cups of Brugal de mallita.
Our sorrows glowing into the chorus
we hoped could be heard by the Gods,
who give light to overcrowded apartments
with overdue bills and pull the night
across skies, sullied and starless,
as our feet kept count.

My Spanglish

My Spanglish carries a Gillete under her tongue,
ready to cut you if say she is the sister of ghetto Spanish.
My Spanglish drops the -s and makes it ma' o meno',
switches the -r with the -l pa' no botal la suelte,
trills her rrrrrrrs cuando tiene un pique rastrerrrrrro,
and if you question the placement of her accent marks,
she will replace them with side-eye.

My Spanglish gets in trouble for falling asleep in church
and winking at altar boys.
Climbs the fence at High Bridge pool to swim after hours.
My Spanglish burns her eyeliner with a lighter before applying it.
My Spanglish can't stop sucking her teeth.
My Spanglish knows the difference between coquito and límber,
pastelitos and empanadas, frío frío and piragua.
Knows how to carry the weight on her thighs not her shoulders.
My Spanglish cooks farina, tembleque,
habichuela con dulce, arroz con leche—
calls it all comfort food.

My Spanglish knows, like lemonade, tamarindo
was a popular drink and it still is.
Knows every Prince, Héctor Lavoe
and Fernandito Villalona song by heart.

My Spanglish wants to be called sexy, not cute.
My Spanglish wants to be called smart before sexy, not cute.
Wants to be called beautiful, like the blanquitas
her ex parades around the hood
to show how he has moved up and on.
My Spanglish mends her broken heart
with bachata cortavena de Frank Reyes.
Se emborracha con boleros del Buki.

My Spanglish always claps when the plane lands safely.
My Spanglish thinks *fre'ca, presentá* y *malcriá* are all compliments.
Married her cousin to help him get his green card.
Doesn't let her kids sleep over anyone's house.
My Spanglish has crooks and cops sitting at the same table
at her daughter's quinceañera.
My Spanglish has a college degree and earned summa cum laude
in resting bitch face while riding the 2 train.

My Spanglish is Washington Heights
before the gourmet fruit markets replaced C-town.
Before tomándose una fría in front of el building
playing dominó con los panas was loitering.
Before *The New York Times* and transplants from Minnesota

discovered pega'o on Buzzfeed and renamed it *stuck pot rice.*
My Spanglish is Inwood
before it became more affordable than Williamsburg
and was renamed Northern Manhattan.
My Spanglish spray-painted over billboards
trying to rename El condado de la salsa *the piano district.*
Wonders if it would have made more sense to name us—
The bomba y plena district
The home of hip-hop district or
The boogie down district
but my Spanglish is certain the Bronx
has always been and will forever be ART.

My Spanglish knows a fire escape is also a terrace.
My Spanglish knows there is no way to heal without—
sana que sana culito de rana.
Can't tell stories about el campo in translation.
Can't flirt using proper grammar.
My Spanglish knows there is no other way to say—
Cónchole papi, you look good!
My Spanglish has a Tía sin papeles.
My Spanglish has a Tía that works in a factoría.
My Spanglish has a Tía that takes care of neighborhood carajitos.

My Spanglish will never call herself broken.

My Spanglish is an unwanted child who insists on being born.
She is huérfana crying an unpaid debt
of commonwealth to mainland lost in a promesa.
Leche cortá of impoverished madre patria and starved island retreat.
She is the unruly second-generation daughter
of un-American and un-standardized.
She is the endangered tongue of a sanctioned homeland
and un barrio cabrón.
My Spanglish is always trying to create a bridge
connecting Quisqueya, Borikén y un verano en Nueva Yol.

My Spanglish is a scared seven-year-old
in an English-only class,
where Ms. Marcy tells me to sit in a corner
every time my tongue resists pressing *ju* into you and *jes* into yes,
insisting Mami's homemade lonches are better than cafeteria food,
certain that standing on el rufo is the only place I have ever seen stars.

My Spanglish has an Abuelito whose primary language
is storytelling, but she doesn't have the time to sit and listen.
My Spanglish can't understand all his consejos,

but feels exactly what he means
when he says, *Te amo, te amo all the way.*

Nicknames Tía Gave Her Nieces When We Reminded Her Of Her Youth

Enero: sinvergüenzas forced to keep resolutions
their parents made

Febrero: bleeding hearts for boys
who never remembered their names

Marzo: atrevidas who seduced spring weather,
braless, in spaghetti straps

Abril: perennials that bloomed best
when surrounded by weed and tígueres

Mayo: half-answered prayers
that looked too much like their fathers

Junio: palomas in heat perched on fire escapes
learning to smoke Newport Lights

Julio: illegal fireworks bursting in the night's sky
on Audubon Avenue

Agosto: shadows in red lipstick
sneaking out during summer nights

Septiembre: dolores de cabeza and stretch marks
that never faded

Octubre: brujitas who wore many masks
and were haunted by ghosts named Tío

Noviembre: memories of absent fathers
who were alone for the holidays

Diciembre: mirrors of Mary Magdalene
who refused to keep their legs closed

Mala Maña: Look

It matters what you call a thing
—Solmaz Sharif

14
Alejandra asked everyone
to call her Alex.
Eso es una vaina
Americana Tía said.

15
Alex refused to wear
a dress to her quinceañera.
Esa es la moda
de hoy Tía said.

16
Alex returned from el salón
with a skin fade.
El pelo le crece
de nuevo Tía said.

17
Alex was rumored
to have tongue kissed Wendy.
Eso es una
mentira Tía said.

18
Alex taped her breasts
down under a sports bra.
Porque son
grande Tía said.

19
Alex yelled, "LOOK
AT ME! I'M YOUR SON!"
Eso es una
mala maña Tía said.

Mira, eso se te quita.

II
Slow Burn

Why I Wasn't Allowed To Play With Boys

By the time my new breasts bounced in oversized T-shirts
Elvin bragged of peach fuzz sprouting above his upper lip
Soft signs of curious bodies, an awkward innocence
Intent on looking for ways to press each other into play
To let fingers tangle in locks of hair, slip and slide into
Opened zippers and back pockets of my tightest jeans
Stairwells and stuck elevators stealing time

Eager and blooming, our tongues abandoning red
Skittles and pink bubble gum in the mouth of the other,
Craving a new kind of chaos from a body learning to
Open and lean into collar bone, savoring a tender
Neck, lacing it with plum hickies that mark territory
Daydreaming of slow grinding on rooftops, breaking night
In whispered conversations, stretching telephone cords
Down hallways, listening for light breathing, asking
O*ye, are you still awake? You still there?* Saying goodnight
So many times, the night taps out and the sun stretches over us

An I For An Eye

I used to take the eyes out of Barbie dolls/blackened them with Sharpies/ wondered why everything blonde blossomed to gold/why everything Brown pronounced broken tongued/spiked in mud/all my Gods are the color of mud/moonless nights/molasses/wet coffee grinds/Black-eyed peas are sacred/the Black: an eye/sight is granted/seen & be seen/I used to press Black-eyed peas into sockets of my knockoff pink Kewpie dolls/Cupid's alter ego/gifted to keep me out of trouble/unseen/unheard/ Cupid: an armed notorious trickster/Kewpie: weaponless quiet sister of an archer/the peas rotting into the doll/Mami yelling/I: seen/Sharpies: a bow and arrow/Black-eyed peas: oculus of luck & precision/my eyes: a starless night ensconced in the clicking of my tongue/my third eye: a galaxy of storytelling/to adjust to darkness: just cover your eyes/to see me: press thumbs to eyelids

& let me speak.

Boca Grande

I have always been called *¡Boca Grande!*
My imagination too loud
for our small two-bedroom apartment.
My singing solos into the hairbrush, too intense.
Roared high-pitched monologues
on make-believe stages in the living room,
until the stern look of adult eyes drowned my speech
¡Cállate! ¡Baja la voz, niña!

Silence has never been in my nature.
Roared in my mother's belly,
conceived from her desire, I was her wish,
her prayer, her first spoken word.
Born to the sound of thunder.
To whisper to the dead, to shout to the living.
I was born to make noise!

To rattle shells, to beat drums,
to chant, to dance, to dream in free verse,
to bless and to curse—
¡Porque Mami dijo que así es que se reza!
I may be too boisterous
for church pillars and Corinthians,
but I got the perfect pitch

for Areytos, Powwows, and Bembés,
and God reassured me,
she speaks my language.

¡Boca Grande!
Wear that title proudly.
Use it to juxtapose the mantra
fed to me by inferior boys who feared my sassy wit,
and pitchfork sense of humor,
hoping I would buy into the belief—
Que esta boca es buena pa' mamar y más na'.

As my tone grew a little deeper,
framing itself to fit my womanhood,
I realized I was given this voice, these lips,
to combat my height,
to challenge the limitations placed on my sex,
to reclaim the forbidden sounds attached to joy,
to moan and stretch in satisfaction, cry in awakening,
sing liberación and pleasure in staccato,
give its rightful name,
scream it aloud through the night
¡Boca Grande! pero con gusto.

Many have tried to impose silence
on what was born of light, of blare, of uproar.
To silence the ancestral voices
that surge through my fingers,
form petroglyphs on my fingerprints,
possess my feet.
To re-enslave the spirits
of La Madama, La Morena,
La Doncella, La Taína, La Gitana,
that have walked with me since conception,
whip them back into submission
at the hands of your disapproval.

Do you know the sound of freedom?

It is in the syllables that escape the throats of little girls
who play loud games of pretend and splatter paint on satin dresses.

Freedom:
It is in young ladies called desobediente y malcriá
for daring to talk themselves into a new form of existence.

Freedom:
It is in descendants of Boricua women

whose wombs were made barren too soon
by government doctors cutting fallopian tubes
in the hopes our vocal cords would follow.

Freedom:
It is in the butterflies that grew wings,
despite Trujillo's attempts at making
insubordinate Dominican beauties extinct.
Ignoring the power of the collective female voice
to do more than just soothe babies.

Freedom:
It is in the hands of clandestine teachers
that patiently instruct illiterate campesinos
how to curl their soil-stained fingers
around a pencil for the first time.

Freedom:
Ominira. It is in the mysteries whispered
by Yoruba priestesses that guard sacred songs
and rituals of ceremonies until
we are ready to receive them.

Yes, I am
¡Boca Grande!
¡Presentá!
Hija de Yemayá—there is no taming this ocean.
My voice will continue to ripen, in tune with my body.
Continue to command airwaves
until I can no longer retain a single breath,
and even then, my spirit will rattle trees and ring bells,
and although you may want to dismiss it as—just the wind
I will remind you that even she has a name—and you will say it.

Bring forth the memory of all the women throughout history
who have fought to break the sound barrier,
who have mended their broken tongues,
who will no longer bite their lips,
who will be feared by the same social norms
and proper etiquette
that tried to restrain them,
warning them
of their delicate *¡re-PUTA-ción!*
Esas malditas de ¡Boca Grande!
who refuse to keep still
and be quiet.

Tía Rocio's Advice To Her Nieces About Disclosing Body Counts To Boyfriends

When a man asks where your body has been:
remind him that you were never good at math,
that pure + innocent no longer added up
once you bled and didn't die, girl ≠ woman,
and you stopped counting when you learned
you were more than a sum of pulsing parts,
when you discovered the darkest folds
of your flesh could swell to candle
the dimmest spaces of a lover's mouth.

Show him:
You have always been better
at reading.

Haikus For Tía The First Time She Returned To Santiago From Nueva Yol

Hair done/doobie wrapped
combed out as the plane descends.
Let the show begin!

Suitcases packed tight
with Payless shoes and discount
clothes: signs of success.

Her skin/less-sun kissed
Her hips/more-holy language
Her body/well-fed

¿Cuándo llegaste?
¡Casi no te conozco!
¿Qué me trajiste?

Her red manicure:
masking factory work and
graveyard cleaning shifts

Her rose gold jewelry:
—after months on layaway—
catching all the light!

Homesick and weeping
across an ocean/but here:
The show must go on.

She returns to prove
herself phoenix/secretly
burning all the time.

Y Todo Comenzó Bailando

¿Por qué es que todo lo bueno empieza
con un par de caribeños bailando?

That's what she thought when she met him.
Their bodies wrapped in cosa buena y sudor.
El amor empezando con punta fina en la pista.
Todo latiendo en *sí* y sentimiento.

Ella es mujer completa de corazón abierto.
She exhaled a yes, making her body a guide
rather than a border. Her hands a map
of lifelines he must learn to read.
She added his touch to her pulse and call it *Vida Nueva.*
She will teach him that being soft is a compliment.
That the first time she called him *Mi Cielo* she meant it.
That her body is a road map to his God,
y su vientre es una bendición que el se ha ganado.
Bendita sean las mujeres that love as loudly as she does,
bachateando pegaito y rogándole a Dios al oido,
sabiendo que este es el amor que faltaba
para ella y sus hijos.
Creando una familia de merengueros,
cariñosos rumberos, she can claim hers.

El es perico ripiao, ritmo corriente,
como un verano en Nueva Yol,
fuerte abrazo, remedio casero de cariño,
el *can-can, ti- ri- ri, can-can* de todas las fiestas.
His fire is necessary passion for life.
Cuando baila, la tierra tiembla de alegría
y los cuerpos piden— *¡Dame Luz!*

Only he knows how to translate the architecture of her spine,
set his ears to breastbone and decipher
the beating of her heart.
He will teach her, to curl her lips into *Dame*,
so he can respond with *Toma*.
He will teach her that to want
is not to harm and that she is ready,
to let his name and the word *safe* rest on her shoulders,
to let him add her sun to his sky.
He is tabaco y ron, dembow con reggaeton,
potente como Brugal de mallita, con una fuerte sonrisa,
que ilumina calle luna y calle sol.

Y como dicen que—*todo comenzó bailando*,
they will continue to sidestep and strut,

—pasito a pasito, suave suavecito—
letting their bodies lead you
into a perfect combination of one,

porque sabemos que todo lo bueno empieza
con un par de caribeños bailando.

Love Letters For Tío Manolo

sat in the quiet brutality
—Yusef Komunyakaa

Friday nights he'd crack a can of Heineken,
play Las Mejores Canciones de Camilo Sesto,
after coming home from the factory to read
the latest batch of letters his wife sent with
Carla who just got her visa. She complained
the letters made her purse heavy. She didn't
want them in her luggage for fear the
blocks of queso Geo and bottles of Brugal
would overpower the Maja perfume misted
over the envelopes. Each letter, a plea
for mercy, folded hands to chest, knees sore
from endless prayer. Rolled from under
the pressure of her ballpoint pen: *perdóname,*
mi corazón es tuyo, te extraño, vuelve a mí.
Camilo's crooning broke the brutal silence
that heavied the air of Tío's rented room.
Each letter ending with a pink lipstick kiss.
The same shade he found on his better-looking
brother's neck the night he caught them coiled
between streetlight and shadow. None of her words
ever made the swelling of his right knuckle

go down. Her nose recast in one swift crack.
Lost between each sentence until the sunset pushed
itself through the opened window. Camilo's voice
a vigil as Tío Manolo held each letter over a lighter,
her lipstick: dancing to smoke.

When Tía Teaches You How To Keep Your Man

She said: *Men only need two things—La comida y el culo*
between drags of a Newport cigarette that balanced casually
between fingertips knowing everything in a country foreign
to your touch is temporary. Always trying to eat
but never fed to satisfaction.

Tía: An ephemeral stream that feared anything outside
her five-block borrowed country. Her section-8 sky grayed
by the barely there rays of a New York City sun
that she could never imagine warming
her childhood home in Santiago.
That sphere of fire dulled among the rooftops
couldn't bronze her skin even in summer. She laughed.
Bragged about her stove having more passion than Helios himself.
Cursed a *coñazo* at the impotence of small Gods
in this great city that watched newly arrived Cibaeños
and Dominican-Yorks dance bachata to the same rhythm
of a new world caught in their cold smiles.

She licked the sweat beading off the brow of her lover
who married her cousin for papers between pulls of her cigarette.
Pursed her lips the same way she had done when she arrived
carrying an avocado seed in her mouth past customs.
No one cared to hear her voice anyway.

Mothering was as foreign as English, but she continued
to summon her womb, pushing forth the weight
of five mouths her hands couldn't quiet.
Their bellies tied to her own empty.
Bottle after bottle. First milk then water.
Lover after lover. First wind gust then ghost.
No one wanted her fracture, her undone seams
of a body with too much to say
and nothing but a fist to say it with.

Men were the only animals she couldn't slaughter
in her two-bedroom apartment
where live poultry met its end
on the kitchen counter every Christmas.
So she held their throats during sex.
Bucking to the pulse of carotid arteries.
Her spine singing perico ripiao.
The warmth of his jaw caught in her fingernails
reminded her of eating ripe mangos
en la marquesina of Abuela's casita.
The juice marking a slow sway down her chin.

Tía: Always hungry, always looking to be fed,
cooked enough to feed all the married men in her building,

knowing there are three ways into this country—
water, wind, and wound.

Learning To Float

When Joel arrived from the airport
speaking only Spanish and still

smelling like limoncillos, his salt
water smile and bronze skin sang

luminous under streetlights, his
swimmer's body caught the gazes

of all the girls sitting on the hoods
of parked cars or popping gum

on stoops. He was the last of Tía Evelyn's
teenage sons to have his visa approved.

After weeks of visiting cousins paled by
windowless one-bedroom apartments,

Joel still beamed, a July sunrise lost
from sea, climbing over the murk of open water

where he fished diapers instead
of flounders. Where a butterfly stroke

interrupted tessellations of trash that
swelled and came to rest on shorelines

next to abandoned fast-food trays and
emptied beer cans spread across sand.

Joel, who beat back any earth in search
of waves, sank until he was risen by the

holy water on women's thighs. Sampled
the reservoirs offered by Barbara and

her best friend Kathy. Learned to trace
the pink and brown tides of Veronica

and Lucy. With index fingers he marked
the moon cycles of Cynthia and Angie.

Set Pamela and Lita's mouths to his
seawater and made them swallow.

His sorrow salting the corners of
their mouths, his body bucking,

trying to stay afloat.

Radio Bemba

He said: Mari cried like I was her first, but I doubt it
She said: I never knew boys could have so many teeth

He said: Sandra was saying no but them thighs said yes
She said: His fire lives under my skin, I collapse to ash

He said: Tanya liked her face pressed against the wall
She said: My body has grown borders named by him

He said: Lucy screamed so loud I covered her mouth
She said: My world was swallowed by his calloused hands

He said: Yahaira passed out after three shots of Brugal
She said: Better to have no memory, no history to retell

He said: Evelyn left scratches all over my back
She said: I can't seem to stitch tender back into my chest

They asked: *What was she wearing?*
They asked: *Why was she out so late?*
They asked: *¿Quién la manda?*

Tía Veruca said: *Agarren sus hijas—que los perros andan suelto*
Tía Antonia said: *Con la boca y piernas cerrada—se ven más bonita*
Tía Marta said: *No eres la primera—no será la última*

she said: ~~no fue mi culpa~~
she said: ~~no fue mi~~
she said: ~~no~~
she said: ~~no…~~
she said: ¿sí?
she said: sí
she said: sí fue mi
she said: sí fue mi culpa

In Leticia's Kitchen Drawer

A Craftsman curved claw hammer to crack coco
and hang portraits, a tape measure to remind her waist
she eats mangú too often, fifteen scattered rusty pennies
to help Tito with math homework or sink into a nine-day
candle to cut Doña Elsa's evil eye on any given day,
five slightly bent nails pulled from the living room wall
that held portraits proving they danced merengue once,
a red silk ribbon to tie his picture to her sweaty discount
store underwear to keep him from falling back into
Tanya's bed, wrinkled menus from the Goodie-Goodie
Thai restaurant on Cruger she treats herself to when
her sister mocks her for never getting a passport
or mispronouncing Pinot Noir, or not having any Sears
family portraits, a ball of white yarn to wrap around
pasteles every Christmas or to secure lucky leaves
above the doorway when he drinks both their paychecks,
film from an outdated Kodak she won't develop to avoid
seeing the exact day she lost her looks on his knuckles,
ginger candy from the Korean market she reluctantly
pushes in her mouth every time he dares her to leave,
every time her tongue lashes a familiar whip to her body,
and when her voice mimics her sister's burn, Diamond
long-stick matches for lighting the broken pilot light
and the candles that keep her bowing to him

How A Wet Mouth Can Drown A Man

Don Ramón, el viejevo of Audubon Avenue, bought us
all Mister Softee ice cream
Every Saturday afternoon, a thick gold chain hanging
from his neck made Tía Belkys
Lick leisurely, vanilla swirling from stiff waffle cone to
glossy puckered lips, their eyes speaking
In a dialect of head nods & deep breaths, the language
of married man & newly arrived
Cibaeña, all salt water & sun-kissed, always hungry,
ready to fruit & unafraid to ripen, her
Index finger tracing the links of his chain, brushing soft
spaces at the neck that made portals
Open, the same way a slow trickle of water can carve
its way into stone, making him believe
Survival without her wet mouth wouldn't last, his
polished exterior dulled in her presence
Other women, he easily rejected, kept his name out of
gossiping mouths, un hombre de familia

Eager to dismiss her as nothing more than a rain cloud,
a tear, unaware that Tía Belkys was
Storm born & relentless, a hurricane with an eye for
papi-chulos who knew how to feed,
Toyed with Don Ramón until he tugged at the line
she cast & buckled under her one
Afternoon, rocking him back & forth like the tide,
his chain now anchored to her neck,
Bochinche from viejitas perched from open windows
threatened to drown him deeper. When
Asked, he denied ever offering her more than un helado,
un saludo, & because water

Easily shapeshifts, crashes & flows, when asked about
Don Ramón, Tía Belkys replied—Me
Lo comí y delicioso estaba—

Why I ~~Shouldn't~~ Write About Mami

There is violence in that love
—Ana Holguin

There is violence in Mami's love/It's a warning rupturing in rage and reopened wound/It's clumsy self-suture when she can't count on anyone to mend her/It's self-taught/It's minimal self-care, second to selfless, and only after the house has been cleaned/It's a problem to be solved, quickly, with no TV sitcom hug at the end/More sensationalized Dominican novela/Less American after school special/But with all the drama to suffer as family secret/It's hard candy with no soft center/It's habichuela sin dulce/It flashes back to summer nights in Santiago where her fight taught boys what *¡NO!* feels like/It tells me *estás gorda*, I need to stop eating/It tells me *estás flaca*, I need to eat/Tells me *que me arregle* but doesn't let me go anywhere/Tells me safety is within her grip's reach/In the center of fist/Under pressed thumb/It straddles me to comb my hair/Trims my ends/Cuts in the name of beauty/Appearances/The look of it all/Her words cut so I too learn to lick/Mend/And depend on no one/It braids my hair into compliance/Burns my clippings to avoid brujería/Fights mal de ojo with an egg/Throws the egg at the neighbor's door/Sends me to church alone on Sundays so people think we are Catholic/Tells me I am just like my father/Loves me the same way she loves my father/Amended/Repaired/Ruthless/Tough and binding/A drop of seawater consistently hitting stone/Hoping to eventually break it wide open/One day/Maybe one day/It sucks its teeth at my lip gloss/Unfolds my mini skirt to graze

my knees/Buttons up my shirt/Tells me boys are not worth crying over/
Tells me she will give me something to cry about/

Asks me who do I think I am
Reminds me who I am/

Reminds me I am daughter first
Storyteller second

Poet only when she deems me so
in front of her friends

Reminds me
I better not embarrass her

Why I Shouldn't Write About Mami

—After Toi Derricotte

She warned me her stories are hers & no one else's.

Says I didn't earn her words.
Says I'm still the unruly child who touches everything that can burn me.
Says her past is an iron door sealed by stone & sea after she left Santiago.
Says I don't know how to slant the truth in her favor.
Says I have always loved Papi more.

But she is the one my muse fears and longs for.
Searches for her like a phantom limb.

Asks me to pull open her bedside table and dig
for old envelopes and yellowed photos.

Asks me to snatch the dust & darkness into light.
Asks me to find her
                    despite—

Stunting

I like the blue nose pit bull best.
How she flexes muscle
and jawline when walking
down Broadway like a bad bitch.
Flaunting a hulking chest, broad-faced
and sleek. Embracing the killer myths
neighborhood viejitas tell
as they cross the street to avoid her,
knowing a pink leash is just
an accessory to her swagger.
If taunted by the tígueres on the corner,
boys playing at manhood,
smelling of Newports and Colt 45,
she will clap back with 300 pounds
of pressure vibrating across 42 teeth
poised for the

What's good?
                    or the

                    You good?
                                    or the
                                    We good?

Somewhere
inside the most tender spaces
in my mouth
lives a bite with a tongue
still smelling of
~~wound~~/wolf.
Grip tightening,
head shaking, unsure
of whose blood
be on the sidewalk.
Ready to stunt
on stories whispered,
~~A bitch~~/this bitch
bred to win.

III
Glow

When That Slow Old School Bachata Sounds More Like The Blues

—After Roxane Beth Johnson

We were the one-hit-wonder
replayed every Saturday night.
Our song of moan, and stretch:
the balm to an urge we wouldn't
name but couldn't deny. How that guitar
soundtracked what only
our bodies could set to melody.
A momentary axis to our rotating
within each other's press and pulse.
An inability to stop the late-night
call and response knowing darkness
swallowed our secret. Moonlight
haloed the licked clean spine, the
bowed head into thigh, the chorus
of *more* and *please* set to a tempo
that grew with each stare. The taste
of your mouth: the hook. Today I found
the scratched CD, sunlight prisming
each jagged line. Rubbed the oil slick
set beneath plastic with the
same finger I used to trace lyrics over

your lips. The song played once,
before buckling—it warned, I still want
everything that wants me.

Tankas Para Las Tígueras Sin Lágrimas

Forgetting to cry,
I drink myself into song
A slow bolero
dragged by my tongue and dark rum,
cut open for him to see

Mujeres don't cry
Yearning, I suckle the wound
Rename it amor
Calling on Mamajuana
to press slow grind down my chin

Hijas de puta
solo lloran de placer
acostúmbrate
Lesson learned straight, no chaser
by men who thought I could break

Why I Avoid Writing About Birds

Mami had three wooden parakeet cages that hung in the hallway of our apartment/Filled them with bright yellow and green budgies/One for each member of our family/Mine was blue/Blue budgies are bred for the pet trade/Not normally found in nature/Beautiful mutants/Tamed and homebound/Never meant to be seen in the wild/Mami's birds weren't trained to fly around knick-knacks like Tía Lety's/Didn't sit on the armrest and learn Spanish curse words like Tía Delia's/Mami's birds made static movements/Plotted in loud chirps each time she opened the cage to replace soiled newspaper/Aimed and lunged past her hand/Their attempts for freedom failing miserably on screened windows and doors that led to other doors/If one managed to take flight in jagged swoops/perch momentarily on the bathroom curtain rod/Mami would gently clip her wings/return her to the cage/The other parakeets went unheard/The subdued budgie puffing its feathers/Mami gently speaking into the cages asking *¿Por qué me quieres dejar?*/The day I decided to leave my parents' house I stole a small dented frying pan/a cracked mug no one would miss/and two soupspoons that had been in my kitchen since Tía Altagracia left el campo en Santiago to warm a cold apartment with plastic fruit in tie-dye glass bowls/and fake plants that wouldn't remind her of death/Mami noticed my clothes were missing when the blue budgie risked her wings/and flew into my corner of the room where the closet door revealed my escape plan/I had already taken shoes/shirts/and jeans to the only room I could afford to rent at seventeen/Rage and disbelief soured Mami's face/The blue budgie and I both circling the room/Mapping a way out/Mami pounced/Missed my neck/and landed on the sofa/Running out the front door rattling a plastic bag full of family kitchen contraband/I learned flight/The birds frantic/Feathers falling from cages/Mami's pain cutting into my stride/Her voice/a cracking/A bird call of abandonment/A fight/A flight/A surrender/All wailing at once/*¿Por qué eres tan malagradecida?*/ My wings intact/My chest rising and falling between sobs/My blue budgie circling the room/Mami's hands ready/To clip wings

When Mami Becomes The Unwilling Muse

Mami's life is a banned book
	I am forbidden to read.

I titled it—Pages of life ruptured or
	Mujer interrumpida or
	Hija de buena madre y un sucio.

Earmarked for a grave upon her burial.

	She prefers open casket
to open mouth.

	Her tongue: where history has died.

Her hands: tight to its neck in case
resurrection is promised.

	In her version, Abuelo's roaming
fingers were a bad habit of dementia.
	His taking of young girls: consent.
The abandoning of bastard children
	throughout Santiago: los días de fiesta.

Some stories were never meant to be told—she grunts

Rewrites our memory, dresses it
in pastel Sunday church colors
even as they bleed out
over Friday night glasses of whiskey, neat.

Proper—that's more her style.
Uses a hardcore stare and the sucking of teeth
to signal my pen back into purse.

Her eyes drain the battery of laptops.
Crushes pages of journals between fistfuls of hair.

Cuenta cuentos—¡atrévete!
Sounds like—*te quiero, ¿right?*
Sounds like—*te creo, ¿right?*
Sounds like words burning
entre la espada, la pared and my chest.

¿If a story is told in an empty campo, does it make a sound?
¿If my story becomes an empty forest, should I make a sound?
¿If cousin Lila's underwear were torn like el campo después del fuego,
should she make sound into a story to tell?

Mami's silence is forest fire where fertile soil still burns.

When I ask if she is ignited in all her stories,

She replies:
¡Sigue echando leña al fuego y te vaz a quemar!

I stoke the fire and she sacrifices truth to it.
Maldice Abuelo's photo.
Threatens his edges with a lighter.

A good daughter is a daddy's girl
who redlines her father's narrative.

Abusador becomes: caballero
Predator becomes: enamorao'
Familia becomes: accomplice

Mami becomes unwilling ghostwriter willing to save face.

I am forbidden to visit his grave.

She knows bones, too, can be read.

Disclosure

—After Angel Nafis

I

Blessing

The day before you died you were both dancing merengue
in the kitchen. Your crotch cutting in close after the turn.
Her high-pitched giggle: a throwback to your fifth date
when she got red-faced off of sherry for the first time
and let you trace whorls down the seam of her blouse.
The cross-stitches marking the spots she designated forbidden
and you—a drunken migrant—wanting to call her home.
You kept the beat as best you could, excess bilirubin
pooling at your ankles, the footwork of a much younger man
who had taught her to enjoy Heinekens from etched glass tumblers
like a lady. Your belly: a reservoir for stagnant blood
and murky waters she routinely wiped off your chin and thighs,
for better or for worse, barring her from a full embrace,
your thinning limbs reaching, marking the end of the song.
You stared at her, in sickness as you had done in health,
head back, mouth gaping open, her wide girlish smile
catching all the light.

II

In Disguise

2.15.16—

> *Mr. Robles Ocasio, Male, 83-year-old, underwent*
> *diagnostic imaging. CT scans and MRI images of the*
> *gallbladder, surrounding lymph nodes, and other*
> *internal organs confirm a malignant growth on the liver.*
> *Growth appears anchored and cannot be removed safely.*
> *Symptoms of cirrhosis are evident.*

Aggressive treatment:
discouraged. Patient should avoid alcohol
containing products when seeking alternative therapies.

Prognosis:
make peace with God(s) as diarrhea, jaundice
and weight loss become belligerent.

Family history:
slurred and gasping.

At patient's request, alternative diagnosis

will be shared with immediate family:
dengue fever, exhaustion common to aging process.

Note:
when daughter from New York calls, inform her
of recurrent nausea, fatigue, and hangovers.

Remember:
sound hopeful.

Pantoum For Papi

From the forgotten shelf, at the top of the closet, your favorite dress shirt tumbles
The smell of cafe Bustelo and anisette rum smother my face
Your sweat, dry, yet still pulsing between buttons and seams
I was told only selfish daughters insist on keeping dead fathers so close
The smell of cafe Bustelo and anisette rum smother my face
At sunrise, your feet shuffle past the kitchen doorway—I don't call your name
I was told only selfish daughters keep dead fathers this close
Even in grief, I am reminded: you loved to take up space
At sunset, your feet shuffle past the bedroom doorway—I yell your name
In balled fists, dark circles beneath my eyes, in my unsteady gait, you linger
Even in grief, I am reminded: you will always take up space
I confess, I want you to haunt me—lounge in every corner of the places I call home
In these balled fists, dark circles beneath my eyes, in this unsteady gait—please, linger
Your sweat, dry, yet somehow, always pulsing, between buttons and seams
I confess: I want you to haunt me, lounge in every crevice of ribcage, call me—home
Each time I reach for the shelf, top of the closet, where your favorite dress shirt tumbles

Why I Have So Many Unopened Bottles of Palo Viejo

I first mourned your death at a local bar.
Every shot of dark rum warning me
of your liver buckling under
years of drunken Saturdays
and recuperation Mondays.

How I inherited this and your passion
for pessimism. A seductive self-destruction
caught in my softest spots: behind knees,
the base of my neck, my ego.

My skin: sexy, red, glowing under the low lights
chased by Jolly Ranchers and double shots.
The sweetest decline to a clear blackout.

My heartbeat steadied only by the low bass
reverberating off humid walls.
I never liked the smell of your Marlboro Lights.
After you left, I smoked all the cigars on your altar.
Made the darkening of my lungs an act of contrition.

The only way to learn to breathe again
was to make it a part of a drinking game.
But I really didn't care if I won or not.

I danced each night of your novena.
Grinding my waist hoping to tempt the fury of a God
I questioned when petitions laid unanswered
under white candles months before your death.

Hoped the sweat dripping down the beads
slapping my chest might knock on a divine door,
hear my calls for mercy, long after your cells
refused to stop amalgamating into abnormal masses
settling on your strongest spots: lower back,
upper chest, your addiction.

Each pulse pushing me past this and every other night.
My body insisting on burning itself bright,
like a good daughter, holding vigil.

Ode To The Necessary Distance Between Us

we love better from afar
our calls are short and sweet
used to think this was wrong
daughters are supposed to care
for mothers whose bellies grew
divided by linea nigra, but mine—
never faded, together we learned
not all borders are partitions,
not all lines divide, some frame,
others hem, some define the edges
so we can decide what to draw
and when to call it a draw—a tie
a truce, knowing when I have gone
too far, knowing I can't change
you—we settle, praising the distance
I have named peace, enough for
you to be daughter, for me to be m(other)

you always say I talk and walk too fast
never run away but sprint far enough
feet always searching for a new path but
you remind me to look backward, a lesson
in shock and sway, jolt and swing, I was always
a lover of dark things, independent, stubborn,
being somewhat separate is best for both of us,
you cut the umbilical chord = we both breathe
allowing us to make space, we shift, while
we find our way back to ourselves and each other
mend, speak-easy, realizing when to hang up
when I chose flight over fight, my exit strategy is
like a lost signal, a button straight to voicemail
I can't be the daughter you want me to be, I fail
time and time, again, but always cycle back to what
both of us can safely say—we still need each other
and for me to be daughter and you to (mother)

Question From My Adult Self:
—What was Mami searching for when she had me?—
With An Answer To My Younger Self

Mami wants a second chance at womanhood/A way to get it right/
Envisions me a newer version of herself/Mami 2.0/La versión
Americana /La hija de su madre/Hija de sus sacrificios/Wants me
to open eyes wide to the city of possibility she immigrated to/
Wants me educada/una profesional/Smile/Hide my teeth/
Busca oportunidades/Don't rock the boat/Don't make waves/
Don't ask too many questions/Don't even think of piercing
your belly button!/Reminds me *Yo vine en avión no en yola*/
Be obedient/*Cierra la boca y las piernas*/*Abre la mente
y los oidos*/*Métele a los libros, no a los machos*/Be "a first"
in this family/Be graduate/Be flawless/Be free of escandalo/
¡Caso cerrado!/Ella ha dicho/Be una señorita/

Girl,

You will question/Argue/ *Why can't I wear these Chiclé jeans?*/
Why can't I go to the block party?/You will be too Saturday night
for her Monday morning/Too fresh CD for her broken record/
Privando en vaina/Try to loosen her grip/Swallow y(our) words/
Level the bridge between you with the friction of a slow burn as you
grind on your crush in the stairwell/*Malcriá*/*Hija de la gran puta*/Roll
your eyes/Quietly suck your teeth/You will build boats
even when you don't know how to swim/You will wear feathers

in your hair and attempt flight/You will complain to your grandmother
about her daughter by candlelight/You will learn to read the compass
she gifted you via the womb/You will become storyteller
always searching for y(our) voice/You will feel like a caged animal
until you become m(other)/Your belly button will pulse the syllables
of her name/Then/You will spend years
rebuilding a road back to her fists with poems

To The Prayer In My Throat

I opened the bag of *Café Don Pello* and out came my grandfather.
Knuckles, thoracic, and lumbar finely ground like table salt.
The colador echoed a décima rising in steam.
A man of shadows, humidity and hill slopes.
        Everything about him makes the sound of sweat.

I drank the cup of coffee and at the bottom was my father.
Loose fist, mosaic of beer and bile distilled into the sugar.
A man of boleros, overgrown banana trees and one last sunrise.
        Everything about him tastes of thunder and black licorice.

I burned the cup over a flame on the stove and out came my grief.
A piercing stain, a chaos absent of light fighting to remain pinned
to a current of intangible knots coming undone. The screeching
of sorrow pulled from my larynx, vocal cords loosening to praying hands.
        Everything about me smells of gut and gash.

How I Learned To Build A Fire

I learned to burn by accident.
Born a fire sign with your quick temper.
The kind that celebrates a burst blood vessel
in the right eye after winning an argument
or vomiting whiskey sour
after a drinking game.

Watched you try to cool a scarred
liver with liters of aloe juice.
A poultice taped to the abdomen
drawing out the firewater.
But every night you burned brighter,
face flushed, a sad clown's mask.

After blacking out in the backyard,
a fifth of vodka shattering
what was left of my forced smile,
I learned to break the fever of withdrawal
with coconut water and real tears.

But the heat of your inheritance
had already scorched
my skin, lightning imprinted

on my back, a warning written
in scattered, sacred asymmetry.

My skin: a eulogy
for what killed you
and died in me.

Your inferno: now kindle
keeping me warm.

Mami Told Me To Put Water Under The Bed

When I was seven: hot with fever,
small pocked body searching for relief,
my chapped lips keeping the beat
of a body pulsing to an illness
no doctor could find.

When I was fifteen: a vessel for an unsettled storm
and growing resentment, my curves becoming razor-sharp
war stories told through the mouths
of boys that had too many teeth.

When I was twenty-three: Abuela's inheritance
of forked uterus and spiked cervix
threatened to scorch my timeline
as it had done to hers too many years,
too soon.

—Water would save me—Mami said

Water would drown out the death
that wanted to so fiercely map itself onto my back.
Poured herself into all the ache.
Replaced the unknown with ebb and flow.

Filled me with a love so hard
it detached me from the fall.

And I came to know water is synonymous
with woman, with warrior, with ritual.
My mouth became a well, a waterfall,
and finally—a weapon, so sharp, so wet,
it could cut the chaos of any curse.

Water would sever my soul from collapse,
free my head of locks too heavy to hold,
reteach my bones to speak survival,
pour molasses into my seams,
and rise as the ocean claims me
as her daughter
over and over again.

Tonight, I will place a glass of cool water
under my bed, listen for the song
of my ancestors that says:

—We would never let you drown—

Elegy For The Last Bottle Of Bacardi

You will always be
	a heavy thirst,
a panting beast,
	a reservoir of cold
sweat blooming
	down my back.
Eagerly riding you
	down my throat
in the evening,
	only to finger you
back up past midnight.
	My nails scraping
uvula the same red of
	bursting capillaries
in my cheeks. My eyes
	surrendering to
a seductive stupor.
	They say
your first love sees you
	for all the gruesome
your naked body carries.
	You licked every inch
of my faded periphery.
	A loyal bitch

nursing the slur and droop,
        the incontinence, the loss
of consciousness,
        calling it all beautiful.

Paper Cranes

Senbazuru: one thousand origami paper cranes held together by strings. An ancient Japanese legend states that whoever folds a thousand origami cranes will be granted a wish by the Gods or hope for a sick person to get well.

On weekends before the usual blackout,
before his stupor went from kind grimace
to self-loathing rage, Papi washed my feet before bed.
Folding three kitchen napkins onto themselves.

Sometimes squares, sometimes triangles, I witnessed
how cautiously the cumbersome fingers
of a maintenance worker persisted in shaping
Bounty towels into sacred geometry, loosely formed objects

he would soak in rubbing alcohol. How he cupped
my five-year-old heel in his left hand and with the right
wiped each toe with the precision of a sculptor molding
a perfect arch from marble. Cuts on his fingers, that took

months to heal, ignored the sting and lost themselves
in the task. The cold on my hallux quickly replaced
by the warmth of his chaffed palm. Dirty footprints,

ignored warnings of running around the apartment

barefoot, marred his disposable boats, hats, and lopsided
long-necked cranes. My sleep comforted by the scent
of this ritual on my feet and the stench of anisette
liqueur on my cheek after a goodnight kiss.

Cleaning my son's feet before bed, he tells me
of the paper cranes he has folded from scraps and hung
around his room. Each one a different dimension,
suspended by strings from the ceiling, perched

on the edge of the mirror or taped to the window frame.
As I massage cascarilla and coco butter into his instep,
he shares his goal of making a *senbazuru*—
his labor guaranteeing us the gift of peace.

Before wiping his feet, I ask him to fold the napkin
into a crane. He warns me the paper may not hold the creases
necessary for a bird to appear. I insist he try and watch
the shadow of Papi's hands slowly emerge

in successive folds and the pressing of fingers spellbound
by transformation. *It looks drunk or maybe he's sick.*
my son declares as the loose outline of a crane unravels
and I drown it in a bowl of water.

Elegy For The Unrecognizable

Science says no two fingerprints are alike
Our genetic codes branded on indexes and thumbs
Personalized identification above the dermis
=
La cédula en la piel

Western belief says my rib was granted to me by a man
This asymmetrical carapace that secures a battered heart,
and shallow breathing lungs is a castaway
A hand me down
=
un extranjero sin papeles

I say I wear Papi like a familiar softness
=
una sábana
=
un peluche

His fingerprints smoothed over by pesticides
picking fruit in Vineland, New Jersey,
or peeled by floor cleaning fluid at the Hilton,
or from wiping away grief too many times
without his children bearing witness

The swirls and spheres of all ten fingers
pressed unrecognizable

I too have fingerprints that refuse
to register with the government
This daughter of a porter by day
and a numbers runner by night
has wiped stubborn ink
from illegible ring finger and pinky
My documents marked "unidentifiable"
The process repeated several times
with the same result
=
I am an unclear, strange being

I say I carry Papi's rib
The left jagged and deformed
Raised as if t(his) heart
was pushing up on it for freedom
=
un corazón latiendo libertad
I lift my shirt to press and show him
the not so smooth bone gutting above my waist
He claims it may have been the result

of Mami craving a shot of whiskey after dinner
A habit he discouraged
but couldn't fight a pregnant woman about

But now that Papi has transitioned

Ashes to tierra,
Dust to monte,
Ashes to tierra,
Dust to monte,
Ashes to tierra,
Dust to monte
=
A la tierra regresamos

I stand here as daughter
=
Receiver of the incomprehensible
and the abnormal,
trying to use the unscientific
and the un-western
to keep Papi close
Learning how to pull his spirit
from my palm sifting through sand

Calling his name and dipping
my unmarked index finger
en una taza de café negro

Tapping my left rib,
calling on the night watchers
to carry the tune
of my bones to his
I'm trying to keep him

recognizable = clear = close

a familiar feeling
I can press my face to
on days I fear losing myself
I know I am the selfish daughter
of an untraceable Boricua,
who taught me how to find him
in shots of lightning,
in bowls of molasses,
in a lunar eclipse
Taught me how to call his name
in toasted corn and crushed eggshells
To pull him from memory

by collecting water in a thunderstorm
I know I am an unclear, strange thing

=

only he knew how to love

When Asked Why I Don't Drink

I say:

- (a) I'm driving
- (b) I'm on medication
- (c) I'm taking a break
- (d) I have a stomachache

What I mean:

Just Dinner, No Drinks

I want to love you sober.
Spotlight each nerve
ending with the last one
you reserve for me
on nights I forget I can be both
lucid and longed for.
Safely on the wagon,
you offer your lips
for days I reach
for the phantom limb
of an empty flask.
Replace bitter schnapps
with the brine of roasted pork
when I can taste the beer bottle
in an old photo more intensely
than tonight's dinner.
My tongue has muscle memory.
You encourage me to sidestroke it
to your ear and listen for the ocean.
You be the water to all the fires
my flashbacks can spark.
You hold the sands of an hourglass
that refuses to go back in time.

Stay in the present with me, you beg
on days I forget how to love
myself,
still and dry.

Burn Me Back

Papi's death was a downed powerline
on an island I tried to candle with breath.
Tried to resuscitate heart with words
screaming into empty palms.
Tried to kindle his flame
with waterlogged match
and empty fuel barrel.

Where can I find his spark now?

I got no fuel left, nothing to tender
his ash and burn mark.
Just this howl like the winds
that follow the eye of a storm
approaching my door each time
I think grief has receded.

Water has always been
                    my savior but now
I summon the rage
                    of a burning thing.

A burning thing that isn't just me.
I need the flash of lightning

that can reignite a nervous system into normal.
Need the gunpowder and smoke of a current
that can scorch me back to him.

Please,
burn me back.
Bring him closer.
Set a blaze

so I can remember his warmth.
I've been told too much fire can hurt,
but this agony be a firewall I'm willing to breach.
This aftermath be hot coal I'm willing to drag torso over.

So let these hands scar
if it means I get to greet
the flash of his smile once more.
Let my body of water dissipate
into mist over mountain,
if it means he comes to me luminous,
like that one star, that one light bulb
that flashes on and off, all night,
          after a hurricane.

Prisms

Papi,
your selfish daughter remembers today is your birthday.
        Did you reach for the red rose I placed in Yemaya's hands?
        Did you hear my chest ignite and bloom at the shoreline?
        Did you feel me inhale the brine left
                on your favorite Yankee hat?

Grief settles in the lungs,
        but since you crossed the Kalunga line,
        I have learned to bite the rage
        and spit it out in small pieces of obi as libation,
        along with the sweet anisette
                that called your liver home.

Papi,
your selfish daughter has not had a drink
        for five years and four months,
        but I can still taste the rim of that last shot glass
                I threw at the kitchen wall.

        How elegantly shattered glass can shapeshift
        into thousands of reckless prisms.
        The soles of my feet softly bleeding
                into each ray of light.

My kitchen is too familiar with blood streams
and the tapping of bones.

Papi,
Tell me again
how I can hear your voice in the red
of every rainbow forced from rupture.

Tell me again
that all birth requires blood, and that rebirth
yearns for salt water, honey and dark rum.

Tell me again
how the ocean places the blue of my songs
in your palms.

Tell me
if you heard me exhale.

Acknowledgments

Gracias/Thank you/Modupe/Hahom

To The Foundation:

Maferefun Egun, Maferefun Orisha, Maferefun Elegua, Maferefun Yemaya hoy, mañana y siempre, Kabiosile Chango, Maferefun Babalú-Ayé, Con licensia Zarabanda, Bendición guías espirituales, santo mayores y menores. Luz a los seres Indígenas—Han-ha'n catu! Bendición Iya Odusinya Jacqueline Martin, Iya Abebelokun Linda Evans, and Obá Bí Danny Rodriguez.

To The Bones And Breath:

Ibaye Baye Tonu-Papi Pedro Robles—Siempre dentro de mi, de corazón a raiz. En vida—Mami María Domínguez Acosta—Mi salvación, mi esperanza y mi fe.

To The Heart:

Los que más quiero en este mundo—Jorge Alvarado, Shanice Robles, Indio Alvarado-Robles, Nauel Alvarado-Robles, Dyani Medina-Robles, Carmelo Domínguez, Denise Domínguez, Jovanny Ramos, Stella Lee, Janina Guerra Arias, and Joshua Alvarado.

To The Hands:

Ricardo Maldonado, Urayoán Noel, Yesenia Montilla, Carina del Valle Schorske, Denice Frohman, Nicholson Billey, Latasha N. Diggs, Willie Perdomo, Sandra María Esteves, Ariel Francisco, Starr Davis, Darrel Alejandro Holnes, Roberto Carlos Garcia, Thomas Fucaloro,

Dr. Melissa Castillo-Garsow, David Tomas Martinez, Nivea Castro, Major Jackson, Sheila Maldonado, Elizabeth Doud, María Luisa Arroyo, Dahlma Llanos-Figueroa, Iris Morales, Myrna Nieves, Jorge B. Merced, Lupe Mendez, Jasminne Mendez, Raina J. León, Yosimar Reyes, Ivelisse Rodriguez, John Murillo, Nicole Sealey, Martín Espada, Marwa Helal, JP Howard, Massiel Alfonso, Lisa "Rubi G." Ventura, Caridad "La Bruja" De La Luz, Nicco Diaz, Ron Kavanaugh, Noel Quiñones, Karla Cordero, Néstor David Pastor, Shihan Candy Warixi Soto, Kasike Jorge Baracutai Estevez, Maritza Feliciano-Potter, Gypsie Running Cloud, Susana Praver-Perez, Janel Cloyd, Reyes Ramirez, Luivette Resto, Daphnie Sicre, Aimee Nezhukumatathil, TJ Young, Dr. Jason C. Méndez, Omar Iloy, Lola Rosario, Matt Haller, Staysi Rosario, Vanessa Chica, Tamara G. Saliva, Katalina Rodriguez, El David, Latanya DeVaughn, Angy Abreu, Karina Guardiola-Lopez, Rebeca Lois Lucret, and my entire poetic and artistic community for the push and pull. Bryam Jiménez mil gracias for the cover art.

To The Places:
The Dominican Republic, Puerto Rico, El Bronx, Washington Heights, the fire escape, broken elevator, and dark stairwells of 500 West 175 Street, the love that grew in apartment 47, High Bridge Park, Coney Island, Orchard Beach, la bodega de la esquina, and the memories that still live there.

To The Spaces:
Gratitude to the organizations and institutions that welcomed my poetry—The Jerome Hill Foundation, The Bronx Council on the Arts,

CantoMundo, The Frost Place, Cave Canem, The Ashbery Home School, Women Writers in Bloom, Dominican Writers Association, Nuyorican Poets Cafe, Desert Nights Rising Stars Writers Conference, NALAC, Caribbean Cultural Center African Diaspora Institute, Higuayagua: Taíno of the Caribbean, VONA, 41st Wildwood Writers' Festival, The Dodge Poetry Festival, BxArts Factory, Candela Playwrights, The Dramatic Question Theater, The PlayGround Experiment, Pregones / Puerto Rican Traveling Theater, SolFest Latiné Theater Festival, Dramatist Guild Foundation, Lehman College, Pratt Institute, Creatives Rebuild New York, and MAP Fund SPA Program.

To The Publications:
Deep gratitude to the editors of the following publications for giving earlier versions of these poems a home or a microphone—*Poem-a-Day*, Poets.org, *The Slow Down*, *great weather for MEDIA*, *The Breakbeat Poets Vol. 4*, LatiNext Haymarket Books, *What Saves Us: Poems of Empathy and Outrage in the Age of Trump*, Northwestern University Press, *Poetry Unbound Anthology*, Red Sugar Cane Press, *¡Manteca!* an Anthology of Afro-Latin@ Poets by Arte Publico Press, *Pán•o•ply: Inaugural MultiCreative Anthology*, *Big Other Puerto Rican Writers Folio: A Hauntology*, NaPoMo American Sign Language Day Video Poem Collaboration, Pigeonpages.nyc.com, *The Acentos Review*, Poetry Centered Podcast at The University of Arizona Poetry Center, Tribes.org, *Kweli Journal*, *The Atticus Review*, anmly.org, *The Common*, Poetry Society of America, 92Y.org #wordswelivein, *Narrative Northeast*, *Mom Egg Review*—Praise Poem Folio, and *Dear Yusef—Essays, Letters and Poems For and About One Mr. Komunyakaa*, Wesleyan University Press.

To Martha Rhodes, Ryan Murphy, Hannah Matheson, Bridget Bell, and the entire Four Way Books family: I am immensely grateful for every single step.

To The Keeper Of Roads:
I am listening.

To The Shapeshifters:
I understand.

To The Girl Who Survived All The Family Parties:
Vamos de mano.

To The Woman Who Remains:
Adelante.

About the Author

Peggy Robles-Alvarado is a Jerome Hill Foundation Fellow in Literature, a three-time International Latino Book Award winner, and a BRIO award recipient. She has earned writing fellowships from CantoMundo, Desert Nights, The Frost Place, The Ashbery Home School, VONA, Candela Playwrights, Dramatic Question Theater, and NALAC. With two master's degrees in education and an MFA in performance studies, Peggy's work appears in *The Breakbeat Poets Vol. 4: LatiNext*, *¡Manteca!*, *great weather for MEDIA*, and *What Saves Us*, as well as online in *Poets.org*, *The Quarry at Split This Rock*, *The Common*, *Tribes.org*, and *NACLA.org*. She has been featured at Solfest Latine Theater Festival, The Dodge Poetry Festival, Lincoln Center, HBO Habla Women, The Smithsonian Institute, Pen America, Harvard University, and AWP. Through her 501(c)(3), Robleswrites Productions Inc., she created Lalibreta.online and *The Abuela Stories Project*. Learn more at robleswrites.com.

We are also grateful to those individuals who participated in our Build a Book Program. They are:

Anonymous (5), Robert Abrams, Debra Allbery, Maggie Anderson, Jean Ball, Sally Ball, Adria Bernardi, Richard Blanchard, Laurel Blossom, Lee Briccetti, Anne Babson Carter, Jennifer Christman, Aaron Coleman, Peter Coyote, Elinor Cramer, Michael Anna de Armas, Brian Komei Dempster, Patrick Donnelly, Lynn Emanuel, Joan Frank, Rigoberto Gonzalez, Elizabeth T. Gray Jr., David and Joan Grubin, Naomi Guttman and Jonathan Mead, Beth Harrison, Jeffrey Harrison, KT Herr, Carlie Hoffman, Elizabeth Jackson, Linda Susan Jackson, Marilyn Johnson, Deborah Jonas-Walsh, Maeve Kinkead, David Lee and Jamila Trindle, Rodney Terich Leonard, Jen Levitt, Howard Levy, Owen Lewis and Susan Ennis, Ralph and Mary Ann Lowen, Maja Lukic, Ricardo Alberto Maldonado, Cleopatra Mathis, Victoria McCoy, Lupe Mendez, Mary Jane Nealon, Nicole Nevadunsky, Kimberly Nunes, Cathy McArthur Palermo, Veronica Patterson, Eileen Pollack, Martha Rhodes, Soraya Shalforoosh, Sarah Stone, Yerra Sugarman, Marjorie and Lew Tesser, Reed Turchi, Maria Walsh, and Calvin Wei